THE RÉSUMÉ

In praise of Ana Croniaeth:

'If there was a photo of the trophy for the 'most intriguing book' award, this book would *be* the trophy in the photo of the trophy' – Başka Görüş, *Mail on Wednesday*

'While in prison for a crime I said I didn't commit, this was the only book I read' – O.J. Jackson

'Treat this novella as you would a résumé'
– L. Detterman, *The Inexplicably Late Late Late Show*

'Croniaeth is an undoubted genius' – S.L. Read, *Impartial Review Quarterly*

'We all too often overlook the author's ability to time travel' – *Time (and Space) Magazine*

ANA CRONIAETH

The Résumé

Introduction by
Niemand Wichtig

This first edition published in 2016 by Gwnewch Credwch Books, a subsidiary of ForLP Publishing and Simon L. Read

Copyright © The estate of Ana Croniaeth and/or Simon L. Read, 2016

Cover Design by ChonX Tombola III

Introduction copyright © Niemand Wichtig and/or Simon L. Read, 2016

The moral and immoral rights of the authors have been asserted

Worldwide theatre release in 1994 by Ffug Entertainment

South Wales Library Cataloguing-in-Publication Data
A catalogue record for the book can be provided via Morse-code request to the South-East Wales Library

Any likeness to persons/situations, living or dead/fictional or real is merely a coincidence.

No part of this publication may be reproduced, distributed, or transmitted in any form or by any means, including photocopying, recording, or other electronic or mechanical methods, without the prior written permission of the publisher, except in the case of brief quotations embodied in critical reviews and certain other non-commercial uses permitted by copyright law.

ISBN-13: 978-1537172934
ISBN: 153717293X

Printed and bound somewhere by machines.

INTRODUCTION

By, film historian, Niemand Wichtig

To understand the origins of this book, we must review the time it seeped into public consciousness. In 1990, cult film director, Twyll Enfawr, was engaged in the throes of filming *Super Cub Scout Mountain*. It proved to be a commercial flop at the international box office upon its release in 1992. It was after filming had completed, at the northernmost base of the highest mountain in Wales (Snowdon), that Enfawr claimed to have found a book from the year 2016, written by Ana Croniaeth. Following what he described as copyright issues 'too confusing to discuss', Enfawr announced he would be adapting the book into a film.

The Résumé: The 1994 Film of the 2016 Novella was initially released in cinemas as a silent movie. This was due to the production team's failure to meet the deadline for sound editing. The great Chilean director and screenwriter, Al Abado, famously said, "I could not believe what I was witnessing" and the film, although not breaking any ticket records or turning a profit, was unanimously adored by us silver screen ogres.

As the first ever live-action film to be created entirely using the stop motion technique, *The Résumé* was widely commended for its innovation. Revolutionary as it was, the film remains infamous for the stories surrounding its controversial and laborious creation. According to various crew members, scenes would be filmed in a non-chronological order, resulting in re-visiting certain locations weeks apart to film scenes which, in the final running order, were back-to-back. Actors were, from scene-to-scene, frequently required to fill in for other actors and, in possibly the most damaging method, nobody was told when the cameras were rolling. As a result, the cast and crew frequently lost touch with reality. This was to take a dire, long-lasting toll on lead actors, Tomas Cravolta and Jonny Truise.

Six months after its theatrical debut, when it was released on VHS, sound was added and, for the first time, audiences around the world were able to experience the script without needing to lip read. Soon enough, everybody was walking around offices and streets and homes and schools repeating the many catchphrases made iconic by Cravolta and Truise.

"Are you questioning my résumé?" people would ask.

"You *__DON'T__* question the résumé!" would be the response.

Lauded as the cinematic release was, the additions in the VHS version added tremendous depth to the characters and plot. Ten years later, in 2004, a DVD version would be released with all new bonus features, including:

- the infamous boat scene (with Australian dubbing)
- end credits (with commentary from the entire cast and crew)
- a tour of Cravolta's personal jumbo jet
- the final 15 minutes of the film (not included in theatrical or VHS releases)

Years after the DVD release, on the social community website *BlueditSpace*, a fan of the film posted their discovery of these bonus extras also being accessible on the original VHS versions by removing the tape from inside the cassette, flipping it around, and re-raveling it back around the reel.

In 2014, to mark the twentieth anniversary of its theatrical release, the film was screened along the entire north face of the Grand Canyon. The original cast were present for the showing, except for Truise who, rumour has it, was on some sort of intergalactic space adventure with some of his colleagues from the Spaceology cult. During the showing, for $29, fans of the film could be parachuted into the canyon from one of Cravolta's jets, flown by the man himself.

A few months ago, I found a VHS copy of *The Résumé* sitting in the window of a thrift store here in San Diego. I entered and questioned the price. The lady at the counter smiled and said, "Are you questioning the price?" to which I replied "No. I'm questioning your résumé!" she gasped and then we both laughed about it. It was great to see how culturally relevant the film's catchphrases have remained after all these years.

I recently returned from visiting the theme park of the film this novella was adapted from. The moment you step foot in the park, after security have questioned your credentials and concluded the obligatory back-and-forth about your résumé, it feels as if one is back in 1986, of which the 1994 film and this 2016 novella is based. It feels like one is *in* the film. Every detail meticulously reconstructed: the university campus, the incomprehensible statue, labyrinthine corridors, and staircases which somehow lead you back to where you came. It all amalgamates to create a surreal and disorientating atmosphere, befitting the film and book.

Rumours of a sequel surface from time to time, yet they are always swiftly re-submerged by Enfawr and the good people at Ffug Entertainment. If the cinematic experience has taught us anything, it is to live in the past, present, and future concurrently. In this moment, we may not have a sequel to the film, but we finally have the enigmatic author's novella. It serves as a fresh, albeit original, take on a cult classic. It accentuates the avant-garde qualities of the cinematic retelling and faithfully shows how the riveting and absurdist dialogue – which made the movie so quotable – was crafted.

Although the original film made significant changes to Croniaeth's story and characters, the novella you are about to read highlights the degree to which film adaptation is a fitting tribute. This novella tells the story of Ted torX (surname pronounced 'talks'), a detective on a mission to find a mass murderer, who is guided by mysterious forces into questioning suspects. As torX's case unfurls, he attempts to update and maintain his résumé to meet the demanding expectations of society. His life floats on an undercurrent of personal adjustments and philosophical musings. *The Résumé* details a world we consider normal but is, in actuality, as illogical and unpredictable as anything we could imagine.

Beneath the disarming humour of Croniaeth's novella roars a story of discovery and an exploration of the boundaries of purpose.

x

The Résumé

American West Coast, 1986

The sheriff slammed his fist upon the desk. "No! I've been down Fairfax Avenue and I've seen everything there is to see: the shop that sells nothing other than maps of Lexington, Kentucky, the little orphan boy who sings next to the mailbox, and the incomprehensible statue! So... you come in here... into *my* office... and you shout the odds about the Northern district? I've told you a thousand times, it's off limits! It has been for years!"

He wasn't wrong.

"Sure... everybody who's ever ventured in has returned... but they've never been the same again! Ted... now he has remarkable fortitude. Waltzing in here every day and opening his raincoat to show me the goods on offer. Well, I've had it with this forsaken city. I'll lock myself in the closet and won't re-emerge until my demands are met... and let me tell you something, kid. Nobody, and I mean nobody, will *ever* question my tangibles again."

"They might question your résumé though."

"Like hell they will!"

He picked up a portable Gatling gun from under the desk. The sheriff rested it in his mouth and then re-decorated the room a fetching shade of crimson.

I considered following his lead, but some hands grabbed me and I was quickly whisked into one of the interrogation rooms.

"There was another murder last night, Ted."

"The sheriff just…"

"We have a photograph of the suspect and a note from her. She hopes we get as much enjoyment out of viewing the photograph as she did taking it."

"The sheriff is…" I pointed back toward the room.

"Now we need you to hunt this woman down. You're the best in the business, Ted."

They ushered me from the room and into the lobby of the headquarters. I inspected the photo. She had an eye-matching neon blue Mohican and a leather jacket.

The whirring sound of the Gatling gun buzzed around in my head. My teeth chattered. My head rumbled.

Pineapples & Denim

The bar stool supported the weight of my harrowed state. My focus floated amongst the blue and red fluorescent beer advertisement bulbs. The barman stood with his back to me, cleaning some glasses with a rag.

"Can I get a beer?"

He turned and put the rag down. "What will it be?"

"Anything..."

He held the glass he had been cleaning under the counter and filled it with yellow liquid. After he had licked the foam from the top, he placed it in front of me.

I rummaged around in my pocket for my wallet.

He pulled a megaphone from under the counter. "*IT'S ON THE HOUSE,*" he announced, before turning away to do other bar related things.

I stopped rummaging around in my pocket for my wallet.

Everybody had left the bar. I finished the final few sips of beer and stood from the only stool not upside down on a table.

The streetlights twinkled through the billows, signalling another successful launch. My visual memory was successful in yet another headspace hijacking.

[The top of his head exploded like a red and white geyser]

Figuring I hadn't had enough to drink, I walked to the only bar I knew would be open on a Tuesday night.

Entering the *Pineapple Club*, the usual scent of bleach and cheap perfume raided my olfactory senses. The dancefloor was full of regulars. The disco lighting shimmered across their oiled bodies.

"Why if it isn't Ted torX!"

I turned to see my old buddy from the force. "Bruce! It's been a long time. How are... actually, who's this?"

We both looked to the floor.

"He doesn't have a name. Here, you can hold the leash if you want. He doesn't mind... DO YOU?"

The unnamed individual shook his head.

"So, Ted, still on the force?"

"Are you questioning whether I'm still on the force?"

"Sure am."

"...as long as you're not questioning my résumé."

"I would never do such a thing!"

"Good. Yes... yes, I am."

"Am what?"

"Still on the force."

"Nice. Carter still giving you crap?"

"Well... he... he's no longer with us."

"He left too? Big retirement party for him, I guess."

"No, Bruce, he's... no longer *with* us."

Bruce raised a hand to his mouth like a bad actor trying to act shocked. Then scowled and started putting the boots to his unnamed friend for the evening. I patted Bruce on the shoulder and continued my journey to the bar.

The barmaid placed my Bloody Mary on a napkin atop the bar. I removed the slices of cucumber and inhaled my drink through a plastic device known as a straw. Tabasco massaged the back of my throat.

A conga line began to form, fronted by a man wearing a black halter-neck and light blue jeans. He sipped his drink from a hollowed out pineapple. It was the club specialty. I had my Bloody Mary in a glass.

With no intention of joining the human snake slithering through the club, I sat back and observed its components: a parade of glistening chains, tanned bodies, and feather boas of every colour.

...and there he was, at the back of the line, denim on denim. I'd never seen him here before. As the line turned at the far corner of the room, he exited – into the men's room. I slurped up the last of my drink and followed.

The music ended, the lights came on, and everybody flowed from the club like water from a busted dam.

Marlon reached into his denim shirt pocket for a box of matches and lit himself a smoke. His slow exhalations rested on the underside brim of his cowboy hat.

"So... where next?"

"Come with me."

I inserted the key into the lock of my car at the police station and opened the door. Reaching over, I unlocked the passenger side for Marlon.

He fastened his seatbelt as I pressed the ignition button.

"START UP SEQUENCE: ACTIVATED. PREPARE FOR LAUNCH."

Exosphere

Earth always looked great from above. The ability to witness several countries at once is lost on so many. To witness night and day, simultaneously, was a privilege.

"I'm working on a case."

"A big one?"

"Murder. Serial killer, actually."

"Rad."

"Yeah, so they gave me this photo earlier but I haven't been able to give it any real thought."

"How come?"

"Carter shot himself earlier."

"He is okay?"

"No."

"Critical?"

"Dead."

"That is a shame."

Marlon browsed the photograph. "I've never seen this woman before. I'll make a mental note though."

"Appreciate it, buddy."

Marlon began unbuttoning his shirt.

"Did they give you a deadline?"

"It was all so fast. I'm not sure. Don't think so."

"CRIME DETECTED. AUTO-DRIVE TO SOURCE? [Y/N]"

Marlon reached over and switched off the e-guidance system.

Résumé

I sat at the home computer desk and typed up my résumé again and again. My typing fingers transgressed the boundaries of pain until I was happy with what I had pieced together. This particular résumé was looking promising. I was about to save it to a floppy disk but, looking around at the other résumés proudly framed and hanging on the wall, I knew it was the right time to finish this one.

I had written my name at the top and a full employment and educational history below. It was in a respectable black font. I understood there was no room for pretentiousness when writing the perfect résumé and would not let anybody tell me otherwise.

A friend once showed me the résumés in his house. Impressive frames and nice wall placement, but the content was sloppy. How this person could wake up hard in the mornings, I'll never know, but they really needed help. I stayed at their house for thirty-five weeks, editing and polishing their entire résumé collection. I crafted résumés they could be truly proud of, résumés they could've handed down to their children had they not been sterile.

I would not stand for résumé questioning.

Convenience Store

"LANDiNG SEQUENCE: COMPLETE"

The custom hydraulic doors of my red *Ferrari Testarossa* hissed as they opened. My boots crunched stones into the parking lot asphalt. I slid on my yellow framed, lensless monoblock sunglasses.

A chime on the back of the entrance door jingled, causing a nod of acknowledgement from the store clerk. The dark brown wooden panel shelves matched walls of the same colour and material. 1970s soda posters, faded by the sunlight, adorned the wall space between the shop owner's framed résumés.

I approached the till and pushed the photograph across the counter.

"Seen this woman?"

The clerk's name tag read: [MARTEL]

Martel shook his head.

"Okay. In that case, I'd like a pack of smokes, a stick of jerky, and no funny business."

Martel lowered his brow. "Are you questioning my résumé?"

"No, Martel... if that *is* your real name... I'm questioning your ability to run a convenience store."

He nodded, silently, but with squinted eyes. "That'll be... err... six bucks."

"...minus my senior citizen discount."

"Ah, yeah, okay. Four dollars."

His fingers grabbed mine during his pathetic attempt to take the money from my hands. He looked quite embarrassed about it.

"If you see the person in the photo, call me on this number."

I handed him a business card with the emergency services number on it. He picked up the card, then looked at me, then back at the card, then at me again.

"Is this for real? I know the number for the cops. It's only three digits."

"They make us carry those cards. Just call me, okay?"

He nodded and continued analysing the card: flipping it, rotating it, and even holding it to the light.

The door jingled as it closed behind me. A red haze covered the blackness of mountains at the edge of the city. A bunch of teenagers were sat, laughing and smoking, on a wall near my car. They did their usual eyeball rolling, gum spitting, fingers through hair, leather jacket lapel pulling *cool* thing, but that's about it. I had bigger sharks to harpoon.

The convenience store initiated its countdown procedure. The teenagers and I soon found ourselves enveloped in a white cloud as the store lifted from the ground and into the sky, toward the hanging neon moon.

The Desk

The paper fasteners lay, uncurled, on my desk. I had no paper fasteners left so I attempted to curl one back into its original shape. Well, the shape it was purchased in.

Several attempts later, I accepted defeat. Sometimes, even when you really want something, you can't have it. It was not meant to be. It never was.

The window brought inspiration for my day. Teens smoked highly illegal substances down on the street below. This was Marlon's territory, his area of focus. On countless occasions he would bring youths in from the streets. He'd shove them in a cell and leave them be for a few hours. Sometimes our colleagues would go in and give the druggies a good beating.

Other times, Marlon would search the streets for people he could frame for crimes they didn't commit. He once brought in an elderly woman and charged her with a multi-million dollar import of crack cocaine. I guess we needed to address the epidemic, so pinning it on somebody somewhat helped. She was sentenced to death. It wasn't a death sentence, but she didn't have enough years to give.

The window brought other inspirations. Various couples walked hand-in-hand, sipping sodas and pointing into shop windows. I looked at the photo frame, positioned next to the computer monitor. It displayed a photo of my family. The photo was non-existent, as was my family.

I double-checked what month it was on the calendar hanging from the back of the door. It was exactly the month I thought it was.

My paperwork was complete.

The Shredder

The cupboard was disorganised. Several boxes needed to be removed in order for me to find the shredder.

I kicked a box across the room, out of the window, and down to the street below. I'm not sure what was in the box, but it almost certainly contained sensitive information.

The shredder was heavy. They said these would be routinely available in homes across America soon enough. It was a prediction I found to be lofty at best.

It made a thud as I placed it upon the desk.

In strips, it rested. My paperwork never looked so good.

Picking Up

The lawn was neatly trimmed. Ceramic plant pots either side of a stone garden path led to a house illuminated by upward-facing architectural lighting. My father attempted to install some once, but couldn't get them to line up correctly and so my mother had to position them. His attempts made the house look all gloomy and weird. My mother always had the eye for aesthetics. Had she been there, in the moment, and not with the research team in Antarctica, she definitely would have approved of the house I was stood before.

I walked the path and knocked on the door. A young woman hooked her head around the door frame.

"Yes?"

"Hi. I'm here to pick up Marlon."

"Who?" she flicked the brunette fringe back from her eye.

"Marlon."

"No Marlon at this address."

"Marlon? Long hair? Made entirely out of silver?"

"Oh! Mar-LON!"

"Yes. Marlon. You know who I'm talking about now?"

"Of course. He's my husband."

"I know he is. I'm here to pick him up."

"He's not here."

"I don't believe you."

"You're right not to believe me. He's upstairs."

"Great. I'm here to pick him up."

"You said that already."

"Look, this conversation is riveting and everything, but could you please call him down?"

"Yup."

She looked me dead in the eyes with a wide smile on her face.

"Go on then."

"Would you like to come in?"

"No! Look, just get Marlon."

"Why are you being so rude?"

"Are you questioning my amiable disposition?"

She narrowed her eyelids. "I'm questioning your résumé."

"What!?"

Marlon came to the door.

"Hey, Ted. What's up?"

"I'm here to pick you up."

"Yeah?"

"No." I turned and walked away.

The Waterfront

The Earth rotated twice before Marlon and I would sit across from one another, eating lobster, at the *Orangutan Beachfront Grill.* It was called a beachfront grill but was actually situated a short walk away, at the harbour. It was widely renowned as the finest eatery in the Northern district with a plethora of awards to its name. One could say it had quite the résumé.

"Is everything to your satisfaction, sir?" a waiter asked me.

I tried to say the food was great through a mouthful of white flesh. The waiter tried not to look too disgusted or offended.

"...and the lady?"

Marlon looked up. "I'm a man."

A few moments later, a different waiter attempted to relight the candle on our table. I prevented this by explaining why we'd put it out. He told us it was more common a reason than we'd believe. Only, I did believe it.

"I am the ultimate third party," Marlon quipped with a mouth devoid of food.

"Excuse me?" I straightened my tie.

"Well, I'm trying to elevate the horizontal reckoning."

I took a moment to process the situation.

"I understand the individual words you're saying, Marlon, but I am unable to comprehend your efforts to formulate a meaningful sentence."

He jabbed at the lobster with his fork.

"How's the case?"

I puffed out the skin above my upper lip. My moustache concealed a philtrum you could sleep in like a hammock. "No luck. I've looked everywhere and spoken to everyone."

Marlon swallowed a bit of his side salad. "Who have you asked?"

"I looked around the *Super Shop & Mart* on Fairfax Avenue... showed the guy at the counter the photograph."

"Where else have you looked? How many other people have you questioned?"

"Are you questioning my..."

"Not at all!"

"Good."

"So? Where have you looked other than the store?"

"Oh, just the store." I shrugged my shoulders.

We ate dessert. I can't recall what it was, but we ate it. It was brown and cold, probably ice cream. It was brown and cold and creamy. It was definitely ice cream. We were sharing it when Marlon noticed something down at the waterfront.

"What are *those* guys doing?"

Two men were lifting rolled up carpets onto the stern of a boat.

"Perhaps they have something to do with your case."

"...because they're loading textiles onto a boat?"

"Yeah, but what about the dead bodies inside?"

"Please." I loaded a spoonful of creamy goodness into my mouth...

"We should go take a look."

...and swallowed. "You should stick to booking petty crooks."

They talked on the dock next to the boat as if they were waiting for someone or something. One of them had a beige suit, light pink shirt, and white trousers. His hair was slicked back. He spoke with his hands as much as he did his mouth.

The other guy was shorter, older, had a white beard, and was wearing dungarees with a white shirt beneath. His boots were worn, but in one piece. He leaned against the post to which the boat was tethered.

Marlon kicked my shin.

Neon Boat

We waved goodbye to the restaurant as it ascended into the late night sky. Once the clouds of steam had cleared, the boat re-emerged, yet the two men were no longer at the dock.

The exterior and interior sides of the boat were white, as is the case with most boats for some reason, but this one had neon blue and neon green top surfaces. Its colours, a striking contrast against the dusk dark orange skyline reflecting in the water.

"Hello? Anybody in there?" Marlon shouted.

"No," echoed a reply from inside.

"I guess that's it then, Ted." Marlon began to walk away.

"Where are you going?" I asked.

"There's nobody in there."

I shook my head and turned my attention back to the stern of the boat.

"My name is Ted torX. I'm with the Ultimate Police Force. I'd like to speak with you for two minutes."

"There's nobody here."

"See, Ted. Let's go."

I hand a finger up to Marlon. Which of my eight fingers, I'll let you decide. I shouted back into the boat. "Look, don't play games with me. I'm a former collegiate athlete with a 4.0 grade point average."

"Do you have any proof?"

"Are you questioning my résumé?"

"I guess we are, yes."

Offended as I was, I removed a copy of my latest résumé from my patchwork leather handbag. I took a moment to appreciate the weight of its solid gold frame. "I have it here if you'd like to check."

Footsteps increased in volume: *clunk CLUNK **CLUNK*** and up the stairs they came. The older man with the beard motioned with his fingers for me to hand him the résumé. After several minutes with it in his hands, he turned to the smartly dressed man.

"I can't read this," he said, handing it over.

"Sí! You have two glass eyes, my friend." He smiled at me and then perused my résumé. "People would be foolish to question this!"

I grinned and nodded. It really *was* a great collection of personal accomplishments and it highlighted my skills to perfection.

"My name is Rui but, on this boat, you must call me Captain."

"Sure, okay Captain."

"You're not on the boat yet."

"I know. I was testing you."

"That old trick…"

"…and I'm Boatmaster Harris," said the older man, "…and you can call me Boatmaster Harris as it's my actual birth name."

Marlon stormed over. "So there *was* somebody on the boat!"

"Yes, Marlon."

He wiped his eyes. "I can't believe they lied."

Rui looked directly at me but pointed at Marlon. "From this point on, we do not talk with this woman."

"I'm a man," Marlon countered to deaf ears.

"No problem." I took the résumé back and secured it safely in my handbag. "I'd like to talk with you about a case I'm investigating."

Rui looked me up and down and then whispered something to Boatmaster Harris.

"Come aboard," said Harris.

I took a step toward the boat, but Rui held an arm out to stop me. "You need to request permission first."

"But he just…"

"It's tradition."

"But..."

"Look, friend, you're not coming on board until you request permission."

"Okay. Permission to come aboard?"

Harris thought about it for a moment. "Permission granted."

I boarded the boat and a triangle of handshakes ensued.

"What about my partner?" I asked.

After several minutes of negotiation and a best of seven rock-paper-scissors contest, Marlon was invited into the convoluted process of requesting permission already granted.

Questions and Answers

Marlon and I sat on a plush flame-stitched sofa in a room within the boat. The lamp bulb gave life to its brass base. Boatmaster Harris sat on a stool next to the mini bar while Captain paced back and forth with a glass of white rum.

"So... how can we help?" Captain asked.

I produced the photograph from my pocket. "I'm looking for this woman."

Boatmaster Harris took the photo and pretended to look at it for a few moments. I gestured to Captain. "Could you...?" He took the photo from Harris and gave it a thorough inspection.

"Tell me... what makes you think I have seen her?"

Marlon lurched forward. "We saw you loading..." I nudged him.

Captain continued to stare at me, expecting an answer. It was as if Marlon wasn't even there.

"We've been asking people in the area."

"Can I ask what this person has done?"

"It's a murder case."

"One murder?"

"Look... have you seen her, Rui?"

"Captain."

"Captain, Rui, whatever..."

"Ask again."

"This is a waste of ti..."

"Ask... and you may get the answer you're looking for."

"Have you seen her, Captain?"

"I have not."

The duo laughed until Captain recovered his, to this point, usual poise. "Let's cut to the chase, Detective torX. You want to know what we're doing with the carpets. Correct?"

"Not that we're insinuating anything."

"It's okay. It's your job to check suspicious actions."

"That's right."

Rolled Carpets

Captain took me down a hatch into the bottom level of the boat while Boatmaster Harris watched Marlon. Two rolled carpets tied with string lay before me. They were rolled to their cores and couldn't possibly contain bodies.

"Where are you taking these?"

"What does it matter, friend? You can see they don't contain corpses."

I knelt down and ran my fingertips along the rough underside of the material.

"We have a buyer in Hawaii... if it eases your concerns." Captain pushed open the hatch and climbed back up. I followed.

Marlon zipped his trousers up and Boatmaster Harris stood from the ground.

"We'll be leaving now," I announced.

Into the Ocean, Into the Sky

On deck, we were met by an endless black, as if floating on crude oil. The city: a thin strip of radioactive mustard on the horizon.

"You might want to come back inside." Captain stood with his hands on his hips.

"Take us back to the shore, please."

"I am the ultimate third party," Marlon interjected.

"What was that?" Boatmaster Harris joined us on the deck. "What did you just say?"

"I was trying to realign the majestic forces."

"I am aghast! Argh!" Boatmaster Harris hobbled over to the side of the boat and, before Captain could react, threw himself into the ocean.

"Would you like a drink, Detective torX?"

"Shouldn't we throw him a rope or something?"

"I'm sure the sea life will give his particles a new home." He headed back down into the boat. Marlon scanned the eternal darkness for Harris. I joined Captain.

The rum tasted sweeter than last time. It was pleasant, especially with the added wedge of lime, but could have used some ice. I was once told never to put ice with rum... or maybe it was some other spirit... nevertheless, I was drinking a delicious drink. Captain was tapping icons on a touchscreen built into the wall. I assumed it was a thermostat.

"You might want to call your *partner* back inside."

"I'm sure he's fine."

"If you say so."

"IGNITION SEQUENCE: ACTIVATED. TAKE OFF IN TEN, NINE, EIGHT..."

"Marlon! ...MARLON!"

"SIX, FIVE..."

"...yes?"

"THREE, TWO..."

Marlon sprinted down the stairs, into the room. He sat down and fastened his seatbelt.

"You could have said something, Ted!"

"I was trying to!"

"INITIATE LAUNCH"

The rattling chandelier crystals and cut glassware tinkled beneath the inexorable sound of the rocket boosters. A résumé fell from its brass hook on the wall. I had given it the once over upon arrival. It was full of spelling and grammatical errors and some of the accomplishments were clearly false. I knew full well who invented the light bulb. These guys weren't fooling me.

With the familiar heavy feeling of a quick ascent, I closed my eyes and tried to relax.

To Orbit the Earth in a Boat

The propulsion system spluttered out. Silence. My groin was running at full capacity. Marlon unfastened his belt and then did the same with the one holding him within his seat. Captain stood from the couch and floated over to the minibar.

"Drinks, gentlemen?"

"No thanks," I said, not thinking about how the liquids would stay in the glasses... but they did.

Marlon asked for a strawberry daiquiri, but there were no strawberries on board, so settled for a glass of tonto with a little paper umbrella sticking from the top.

"So why are we up here?" I asked.

"I needed to get away from Boatmaster."

"How come, Captain?"

"Please... call me Rui. We're not on the water anymore."

I delivered a solitary nod of acknowledgement.

"He knows the woman in your photo."

I thought about the man's questionable claims. Perhaps that was why he jumped into the sea. Maybe that explained his reluctance to converse.

"We should go back and find him."

Marlon gulped down his drink. "Where did you get this? It's spectacular."

Rui swirled his rum and directed Marlon's answer at me. "We got it in Uganda while visiting a few of Harris' wives... and most of his children."

I licked my moustache. "We should go back and find Harris. I have questions I need answering."

Rui laughed. "Perhaps I can answer them... now he's not around."

"Tell me what you know."

"What I know you could write on the back of an invisible pixel with a broken pen. Now, come with me."

He put down his drink and opened an air vent in the top corner of the room. He floated inside and we followed. The enclosed space enhanced Rui's aromatic fougére aroma of tobacco leaf and tuberose, classic and gentlemanly. It reminded me of a freshly cleaned old room or a barbershop from back in the blood-letting era. It was comforting, in a trust building sort of way.

The vent eventually opened out into a new room made entirely of glass. The planet rotated below, dark, yet illuminated by the lights of the cities and towns, exactly as we'd left it.

"Beautiful..." we all muttered within a half-second of seeing the black sphere dotted with yellow and orange and red, like a dark chocolate truffle sprinkled in gold leaf. It was a sight we witnessed every other day, yet still coaxed such involuntary reactions.

We exited the glass room through another vent and, after turning several corners, found ourselves inside a black room with green neon stripes along the wall and ceiling edges and a black/white checkerboard floor.

Rui pointed to the corner of the room. It didn't appear anything was there, but I walked over anyway. My fingertips slithered down the wall. It was velour covered.

"What are you pointing at?"

"Are you questioning my résumé?" Rui replied.

"I think he's questioning your instructions," Marlon answered.

Rui ignored Marlon's response but nudged him in the arm. "You should go over and help your friend."

Marlon shrugged his shoulders. The sharpness of his padded shoulder corners created questions not willing to listen to answers. Marlon joined me in the corner.

"Push the wall," Rui instructed.

I pushed the wall. Nothing happened.

"Together," he clarified.

We pushed the wall and a secret door popped open to reveal a bright white corridor with another door at the end.

"The answers you require reside on the other side. Go... find your truth."

Rui smiled and held his arm out, palm up, as if to motion us down the corridor.

"Are you coming?" I asked.

Rui shook his head. "This is *your* investigation."

"C'mon, Marlon."

We entered the corridor. The door closed behind us. We didn't check to see if it would re-open like they do in horror movies. My eyelids knelt before the strength of the lighting. It moved us along.

We reached the door at the other end. It had a calculator taped to it with 'PIN: 9925+9925' written in red marker pen ink on a strip of paper placed above. I entered the pin into the calculator and nothing happened. Marlon pressed the equals sign and the door unlocked. We pushed it open and found ourselves in the alleyway across from the incomprehensible statue on Fairfax Avenue.

Walking Tall

We chose to abandon the car and strolled through the streets toward the *Pineapple Club*.

We walked through the Korean district and then through the market, toward the college. The streets were quieter than usual. The night birds chirped. Ventilation ducts whirred and blew steam out into the streets. We took the open roads and shortcuts through narrow alleys littered with litter and the homeless. Marlon gave a downed individual a kiss on the forehead. He thanked Marlon, but said he'd prefer some money. I turned a blind eye to the rest of the interaction.

A group of students sat on some steps next to the fountain at the college. They sipped from bottles in brown paper bags and yelled amongst themselves.

"Yo, dude," one of them yelled.

We stopped and looked in their direction.

"Could you go to the store and get us some alcohol?"

"You have alcohol, don't you? In that bag," Marlon enquired.

One of them took a few steps toward us. "Yeah, but we're having a party later." He was tall and sporting an official college jacket: dark red, with gold trim.

"You got money?" I asked.

"Yeah." He took a wad of cash from inside his jacket and handed it to me. They were the sort of college kids who drive luxury cars and have their rent paid in full by their parents.

"You want us to get anything in-particular?"

The student turned to his gang of six. "Who's got the list?"

After a small wave of shoulder shrugs, one of them piped up. "Benny has the list. Benny! Hey, BENNY!"

Benny was over at the fountain. He turned and zipped his trousers up. "WHAT?"

"THE LiST! BRiNG iT HERE!"

Benny gave a thumbs-up and then jogged over, pulling the paper from his pocket simultaneously, making him look like he needed miracle hip replacement surgery.

"What are you drinking there?" Marlon asked the student with the brown paper bag.

"Sarsaparilla."

"But that's... that's not..."

Benny handed the list to the tall kid in the college jacket, who then handed it to me.

We turned to leave, but the students dragged Marlon away. "He stays with us until you get back."

"Fine."

"We can't pay you..." They definitely could have. "...but feel free to party with us, yeah?"

I didn't dignify him with a response.

Super Shop & Mart

Getting to the *Super Shop & Mart* required a full reversal of our walk. On Fairfax Avenue, I walked by the incomprehensible statue and the shop selling only maps of Lexington, Kentucky. How that place remained open in a city so far away from Kentucky will remain a mystery. I walked across the parking lot and beyond the jingly door. I headed directly for the alcohol and opened the list:

Party

Beer

Saspurila

Hard liqor

Wisky

~~*Nuts*~~ ~~*BALLZ*~~ *Nuts*

~~*Porno*~~

Ice

Sodas (whatever)

~~*Water*~~

Despite the spelling errors and its juvenile contents, I collected all of the items and cradled them in my arms. I took as much as I could to the counter and then went back to collect the rest. The nuts were attached to a piece of cardboard hanging from the end of the aisle nearest the checkout.

Martel surveyed the items I'd rested on the counter.

"Having a party?"

I nodded.

"This sure is a lot of coquito."

"Isn't that what the kids drink these days?"

He stopped entering the prices into the cash register and raised one half of his monobrow. "What sort of party *is* this?"

"They're students."

"Look, let's just pretend this conversation didn't happen."

Martel finished adding my total in silence. He curled his mouth upwards to scratch the underside of his nose with his thick black moustache.

"That'll be... $22.94"

"Minus my senior citizen discount..."

"Oh, yes. That'll be... 15.30."

I placed the goods in as many bags as it took and made the slightly more arduous return journey.

Hot Tub

"Dude, that's huge!"

I had no idea what they were talking about in the kitchen, but it sounded huge. Marlon licked the creamy beige coquito from his top lip.

"It's no tonto..."

I joined the guys in the kitchen. Some were stood around drinking beer while a duo poured entire bottles of rum and whiskey and vodka and gin into a large bowl filled with ice and topped with soda. The other four inspected a sizable hot tub, situated in the communal garden just outside the kitchen door.

Somebody turned up at the party with a goat.

We all sat in the hot tub. It had all the features: it held water and it held the air it was inflated with. It had *Totally Hot Spring Spa* printed on it. The turquoise text complimented its pink and white body perfectly.

"We need to go get the others," Benny said.

"Nah, dude, they're coming straight here," one of the other guys explained. I had still not discovered all their names.

I asked a few of the students about the woman in the photo. There was one guy who provided me an elaborate story which involved him once being married to the woman, in a different life. They went on honeymoon to Nova Scotia and he found out she had a tattoo around her thigh of every American vice president in history. At this point he began to puke into the sink and I took this as my opportunity to end communications. None of the other guys had seen her before either.

They stepped down the ramp from the spacecraft. Grey, around human height, gangly limbs, and tennis ball sized black eyeballs. They looked exactly like in those Roswell videos.

All three were given drinks and welcomed by the students. They joined us in the hot tub and showed us their individual résumés on holographic projection screens.

Aliens

The aliens instigated several water fights during the party.

The Comedown

The room felt as if it was turning to the left as I sat at my desk making amendments to my résumé. I was drinking coffee. It was a mellow coffee. Someone knocked my front door. I answered. It was a courier. I signed for the package. It was a set of picture frames.

I edited my accomplishments and my qualifications history. There wasn't a lot to do but, as a great woman called Anon once said, '*Judge a person not by their character, but by the quality of their résumé*'

I printed and framed my latest effort and hung it up with the others.

The Paperwork

With the ink levels in my pen depleted, I asked several of my colleges if they had a replacement. Nobody at the station could help, so I opted to use a pencil.

I noted my findings, making sure to omit any mention of Marlon. He had his own cases to handle. Besides, forced on me as it was, this case was *my* baby.

After a full two hour shift, I trashed my office and filed my papers in an upturned cabinet.

Phone Call

I sat at the bar. It had been a long day at the office. My tie was loose, my brain was tired. I was thirsty.

The telephone rang. I told the barman to keep the change as he placed my drink on the beer mat.

My gulps of beer turned to sips. They were showing highlights of the Oilers/Dolphins game on the jumbo nineteen inch televisions scattered around the place.

"Call for Ted torX?"

I held my arm aloft.

The barman covered the microphone. "You'll need to come here. The cord won't stretch."

"Detective Ted torX, speaking."

"*I have information.*" The voice sounded as if they'd chain smoked without pausing to eat, sleep, or breathe for several decades.

"Regarding?"

"*Your case. The murder one.*"

"What do you have?"

"*Do you have a pen?*"

"I do." There was a pad stuck to the wall next to the phone. A pen resided in an attached holder.

"*The woman... she's at the following address...*"

Fifth Gear

The open road: a blue illuminated grid against my red *Testarossa*. The three-hundred and ninety horse power engine purred through the night. The passing road signs and billboards absorbed into the reflection of my eyes.

The songs on the radio, a mix of synthetic instrumentation and saxophones, became the soundtrack to my long drive across the state.

I reeled in the mountains.

The Given Address

I woke up in the front seat. My wristwatch said it was 1pm. The address given to me by the person on the phone was across the road. The house had colourful balloons on the porch either side of the front door. I checked my appearance in the rear-view mirror.

I knocked on the door. Youthful screaming and shouting emitted from within the house. I knocked again.

I sat on the porch chair and waited.

Twenty minutes later, a car pulled up. A man and a young girl got out and walked toward the house. She was holding a box, tied with a bow.

"Your kid here too?" the man asked me.

"I'm a detective. I need to speak with the homeowner."

"Have you knocked?" asked the young girl.

I nodded. They knocked for their own purposes. Somebody answered immediately. Much jovial welcoming occurred. The woman who answered the door jumped as I appeared from the side, holding my badge.

"You startled me!"

"Yeah, whatever. My name is Detective Ted torX and I'm here to have a little look around."

"There's a children's party going on. Do you have a warrant?"

"Everything gonna be okay here?" the man chipped in.

"Yeah... I think so..."

He backed off the porch and waited by his car.

"I don't have a warrant, but if you've nothing to hide, you won't mind me taking two minutes to have a look around."

"Two minutes?"

"...and I'll be out of your hair."

"I guess, then. Come in."

Kids were running around, dancing to music, and creating a cacophony.

"What are you investigating?" the homeowner asked.

"Are you questioning my résumé, ma'am?"

She covered her mouth in horror. "Oh, lord no! I would never..."

"Good... because you don't question the résumé. It's a murder case."

"Yeesh. I'm sure you won't find anything here."

I checked stacks of letters for anything handwritten, I looked under tables for anything suspicious, and I inspected the résumés on display for any discrepancies.

I opened the closet next to the downstairs bathroom. There were two black shoes attached to grey trousers at the bottom. I parted the coats above to find a man with greasy hair, thick-lensed spectacles, and a green raincoat. He held an index finger to his mouth.

"Shussssh..."

"Would you like to come out of there, sir?"

"Not right now. Leave the door ajar, please."

Following his instructions, I went to find the lady of the house.

"Thank you for letting me take a look around."

"That's okay, Detective torX." She pronounced my name incorrectly.

"Everything looks okay here. Enjoy the rest of your day. I'll see myself out."

I turned to leave when something tugged at the knee area of my trousers. A little boy looked up at me.

"I think you left your thing on the window over there." As he pointed, the homeowner picked up the framed paper.

"Is this your résumé, Detective?"

"Ah, yes. Thanks." I took the sheet and stored it safely in my handbag. She did the weird *flappy hands in the face* thing as if to cool herself down. I smiled, picked up the entire birthday cake, and exited the premises.

At Lunch

I ate lunch in the front seat of my car. It had buttercream frosting and an edible number 9.

HQ

My colleague, Detective Oxnard J. Fagby, approached while I was making a caffeinated beverage in the lunch room. He was enormous and his face was almost bigger than his head. His moustache was outrageous. It looked like a sweeping brush. His breath smelled of onion soup. He leaned in.

"I hear you're working on the big murder case?"

"I am."

"I hear you're not doing a good job. I hear they're planning to assign it to somebody competent and, let me tell you, I put my name to the top of the list."

"...and how did you do that?" I took a sip of my coffee. It was still too hot.

"Let's just say I've been kneeling in the men's room a lot this morning."

I stood from my chair and exited the room but, before I did, I shouted back to let him know the case was going great, although, of course, I knew the truth.

Time was of the essence. I input a combination of numbers into the telephone. A sequence of technical events took place which led to the base emitting a sound at Marlon's house. The sound alerted Marlon's wife to the fact somebody was trying to get in touch. She picked up the handset and we began interacting verbally.

"What?"

"Hi. Is Marlon there?"

"Marlon?"

"Mar-LON? Your husband."

"Oh, him! Yes."

"...can I speak to him?"

"Where I come from, people say please."

"Please."

"Please, what?"

"Can I speak to Marlon?"

"Yes, but say please first."

I nearly threw the phone at the wall, but then I remembered Detective Fagby's threat to steal my case.

"Please... may I speak with Marlon?"

"Yes."

Marlon eventually took control of the phone.

"Yes, Ted?"

"We need to talk in person. It's urgent."

A Time to Rethink

Marlon met me at a local diner. He had waffles and I wasn't hungry. I'd brought a full collection of my case findings. He said he'd help.

"So..." he said through a mouthful of syrupy goodness, "...what do you have?"

I gazed down at my coffee. "I visited an address yesterday..."

"You did?"

"...turned out to be a dud lead."

"Ah."

"Yeah..."

"What else do you have?"

"Nothing."

A waitress approached. Her nametag read [MARÍA]

"Everything okay, sir?" she smiled at me. I nodded back. Then she turned to Marlon.

"...and the lady?"

Marlon looked up. "I'm a man."

She continued to smile. "Hey, that's great!" Then she walked away.

Marlon closed his eyes and shook his head before shovelling more doughy loveliness into his body. He chewed, then swallowed, then nabbed his mouth with a napkin before making a solid suggestion.

"I think you need to get into the mind of a mass murderer."

"Easier said than done, Marlon."

"You could visit my mother."

I could not respond with a mouthful of coffee, so Marlon continued…

"Would you like to visit my mother in jail?"

I gulped it down. "Yes."

Marlon's Mother

They asked us to sign the register at the reception, even though we showed them our badges and résumés. A warden showed us to the meeting room where we sat across from Marlon's mother, Marlony.

Marlon and his mother attempted to hug one another and successfully managed this for a brief moment before a guard yelled "No contact!" at them.

We sat one side of a wooden table in the centre of the room. Marlony sat on the other side. Her morbidly obese frame was covered by an orange jumpsuit. Her morbidly obese frame was barely supported by the school-style plastic seat.

"Mom... this is my colleague, Detective Ted torX..."

I dipped the brim of my cowboy hat.

"...and I am Marlon, your son."

"Yeah, I know. What you doing here?"

"Ted here would like to ask you a few questions about your craft."

"Craft?"

"Yeah... you know... murdering people."

She scratched her head. "Does he have any credentials to show me first?"

I opened my handbag and removed the latest framed copy of my résumé. Her eyelids opened to their widest point. She gasped as she lost herself in my employment and educational landscape.

"Can I keep this?" she asked.

"I'm afraid not."

"Is it... real?"

"Are you questioning my résumé?"

"Young man... even *I* know you don't question the résumé..."

"...and *you're* a highly suspicious individual," Marlon added.

"Can I keep this?"

"Again... no."

After intense negotiations, I finally retrieved my résumé.

"Do you know this person?"

I slid the photograph across the table. Marlony ran a flumpy digit down the image.

"Nope, but I get the feeling I do."

"Okay." I took the photo back. "If it comes to you, get in touch."

"Sure."

"Now... if you were going to murder people, what would you do to keep yourself from getting caught?"

Marlony laughed. "Take a look around you, sweetheart. You're asking the wrong person."

I thought about this for a few minutes. We sat in silence as I rummaged around inside my brain.

"...okay, I'm done here." I had failed in my attempt to come up with anything else to ask. Marlon and I stood from the table. Marlon and Marlony enjoyed one quick round of rock-paper-scissors before we left the jail with Marlon analysing his crushing defeat.

Demands

On the way back from the jail, Marlon and I agreed to stop at a bar to write our reports. The news report on the radio said three more people had been killed overnight, two women and one child. There was no trend. The victims were of various genders, ages, statuses, and races.

"Your mother wasn't much help."

"Nothing new there."

The phone rang. The barman picked up.

"That's the last time I take your advice, Marlon."

"Call for Ted torX!" the barman yelled.

I raised my hand. "That's me." Remembering the cord length complications from last time, I slid from my stool and walked over.

"Hello?"

"Detective Ted torX?"

"The one and only."

"Quaint. Now listen up, you limp prick..."

My face made a surprised expression I can't accurately describe.

"...I have the information you need. The information you desire."

"Yeah?"

"...yeah."

Several minutes elapsed...

"Well... what is it?"

"*Ah! Not so fast, Detective. I'm calling the shots here.*"

"What do you want?"

"*Marlon.*"

"Who is this? ...and why did you send me to that birthday party?"

"*Under your stool you will find a blindfold. Place it on Marlon and bring him to the first alleyway heading north off Bork Avenue.*"

"What are you going to do with him?"

"*That's between us. If you want the exact location of the woman you seek, you'll do as I say.*"

I looked back at Marlon, sucking rum and chocolate milk through a straw. I took a moment to appreciate his long silver hair thrashing, and settling, in the gusts of an oscillating fan behind the bar. My eyes followed the path along, then down, the shoulder pads of his white blazer.

"Deal."

"*Okay. Leave him there and, once we've picked him up, we'll call again.*"

"...give me five minutes."

The Drop Off

"When can I take this off? I'm gonna take it off."

"No! You'll ruin the magical surprise I have for you, Marlon."

We reached the alleyway. I stood him under the bottom flight of a steel stairwell on the external wall of the Porcelain Finance building.

"Wait here."

"For what?"

"Please... Marlon... trust me."

"My hair is windswept with trust for you, Ted."

I turned the corner. I did not know if I would ever see Marlon again.

Information

Several hours after I had left Marlon, I found myself still waiting at the bar. The barman had handled multiple phone calls and I sat straight with anticipation during each.

I peered into the green bottle of beer. The remnants trickled down, coating the bottom as I tilted it like a pocket telescope. The difference being telescopes *improve* your vision.

"Where did you go to college?" I asked the barman, pointing to his degree certificate behind some empty wine glasses.

"North Hollywood. Graduated in Bar Studies."

"Bachelor of Science?"

"Ph.D., actually. Doctor Phil Genesis, nice to meet you," he offered a handshake.

"Detective Ted torX. Likewise."

"Your friend... gone home?"

"He's had a long day."

"Shame." *Business or pleasure?* I asked myself.

The phone started ringing.

"...if you'll excuse me, one moment." Doctor Genesis marched to the phone and answered with the bar's usual salutation.

"Ted... for you, again."

I approached.

"You working from here or something?" the doctor half muttered.

"Detective Ted torX speaking."

"The one and only?"

"Yes." He was trying my patience.

"Radical."

"What do you want?"

"Oh, we have everything we want. I believe this call is about what you want."

"Yes, well, what can you tell me?"

There was yelling in the background to the call. *"...did I say you could stop?"*

I tried not to think about it. "What can you tell me?" I repeated.

"The person you are looking for will be at the soup kitchen down on 3rd."

"Soup kitchen, you say?"

"She will be there from two o'clock."

"Excellent."

"Would you like to speak to Marlon?"

"I would like nothing less."

"Well, we weren't gonna let you anyway."

Soup!

Imagine soup. Now you're experiencing exactly what I was experiencing while travelling to the soup kitchen. My automobile provided a luxurious ride.

I knew the odds were against me, particularly if they had allies. I remembered the fortnight of training I did to become a law enforcement officer, and the additional three-day course to become a detective. I recalled the advice given to me by my trainer, Bernie.

1. Make sure you have clean socks and shoes
2. Update your résumé

I was not in the mood to let anybody down. Ted torX had made enough sacrifices. It was time to cash in.

Marlon

Thoughts of Marlon's situation occurred now and again. I pictured what they were doing with him and why they needed him. I was certain he would adjust to his change in lifestyle. '*He's resilient*,' I'd tell myself.

Soup Kitchen

I pulled up outside and dimmed the headlights. The soup kitchen, *Turbo Soup,* was full of soup-hungry soupers. I slouched back in my leather seat and observed.

People at the front of the joint were chatting and slurping and not fitting the description. Servers milled around behind them, and that's about as much as I could see without heading inside.

I entered the building next to *Turbo Soup* and approached the counter.

"Beer, please."

"We're a pet store."

I took a look around. His words were strong and true. They had all sorts of animals: rabbits, goldfish...

...and all sorts of animal snacks: rabbit food, goldfish flakes.

"I'll take a rabbit and some goldfish flakes to go."

"Absolutely, sir." He vacated the counter to collect my rabbit and the flakes.

"They're non-specific fish flakes."

"That's okay."

"Would you like them gift wrapped?"

"The flakes?"

"Can do both if you like."

I shook my head and wagged an index finger.

"That'll be twenty-five dollars and forty-two cents. Let's just call it forty-six."

"Minus my senior citizen discount..."

He handed me my change, a rabbit, and a tub of fish flakes. I exited the store and gave the fish flakes to a homeless man sat in the doorway of an abandoned store.

I marched into the *Turbo Soup* soup kitchen with the rabbit kicking out in every possible direction.

"Would you like us to boil the rabbit?" a grinning waiter asked.

I ignored his idiocy and took a seat. Everybody was happily slurping away. The soup craze had really taken off. A woman tilted the bowl and brought it to her lips. Her long brown hair dipped into the liquid deliciousness. The soup-matted strands slopped back into the shoulder fabric of her beige dress. She noticed immediately and reacted exactly how you would expect a person to react in such a situation.

Searching

I named the rabbit Kicky. Kicky kicked about in my arms. If I had a bowl of soup on the table, he would certainly have kicked the soup off. It was almost a spasm, rather than a considered attempt to lash out at anything.

I sat and thought about the case. Could I be bothered continuing? Perhaps I could discard the case, quit my job, and dedicate my life to freeing Marlon from whatever degrading acts he was being subjected to. I considered what he had become, both physically and mentally. I then thought about ordering some soup.

As I slurped the last of the tomato flavoured liquid, I noticed something written on the bottom of the bowl:

i'M iN THE KiTCHEN, TED

The chair screeched across the floor as I stood. Kicky continued doing what Kicky did best. I slalomed through the diners.

A sign on the kitchen door stated only staff members were allowed to enter. I considered applying for a job, but then remembered the pressing nature of the scenario.

The door swung open. The head chef and several of the soup making sous chefs stopped and stared. I removed the customary from my handbag – which was far more difficult to do while cradling Kicky – and presented my worth. A woman who matched the description of the murderer approached.

"What a lovely rabbit," she said, holding her arms out. She took Kicky from me. Kicky kicked out at her.

"Oooh! I'm gonna have to name you Kicky."

"I already did."

"Isn't he beautiful? Who's a pretty wabbit?" she tickled the underside of his jaw. Kicky kicked the air.

My eyes were telling me she was the murder I had been looking for, but I wanted verbal proof to make certain.

"Do you work here?" I asked.

"Who knows? *I know! I know!*" the latter part of the quote was directed at Kicky.

A ball of fluffy kicking fur clattered into my face. Kicky hit the floor and hopped away in a similar manner to the woman, exiting through a door to the back of the kitchen.

The Getaway

She ran toward the main street. I trailed in pursuit. A white van opened its doors at the end of the alley. She climbed inside and the van pulled away. I caught up with the vehicle before it turned out into the street. I climbed inside and then to my feet, steadying my balance by pushing a palm against the ceiling. The woman was nowhere to be seen.

The back of the van looked like the back of any regular van: four hard walls and a floor. This one, however, had a door on the driver end wall. I opened the door to reveal a corridor. I began to walk down the corridor. As the lighting flickered, my shadow played peek-a-boo with the claret walls.

Labyrinthine

After navigating a series of turns in the corridor, I parted some curtains and strolled into a cylindrical room. An elderly woman played a saxophone while seated on the edge of a small stage. I did not recognize the tune, but there she was, in an off-white cardigan and a floral skirt.

I attempted to talk to her. I attempted to get into her line of sight, but her eyes were closed. I tapped her on the shoulder, but it was hard as rock and she continued without acknowledgement. The raised lettering on the back of her neck read '**MADE iN TAiWAN**' and I realized her eyes were never to open.

I dragged my fingers around the wall of the room until I found a small slit. I nudged the wall either side of the slit until the segment of wall moved. No door sprung from its spot. A buzzing noise emitted and the walls started to spin. We started to move as if in an upward moving elevator. The floor opened up and a staircase, white with black rails, led down to a hallway with white flooring, black walls, and red furniture.

At the bottom of the stairs, a butler approached. She had long, permed, dark hair and a monocle. "Would the gentleman require anything?"

My eyelids narrowed.

My palm covered the brass handle to the front door.

"I wouldn't..." the butler warned. "The person you are looking for is through there." She pointed to a vent just above the skirting board next to a black plywood cabinet. The idea of environmentally considerate design had really taken off.

I took a piece of paper from my pocket and used the origami skills acquired in detective school to form an airplane.

"Climb on," I said to the waitress.

We taxied around the hallway until lined with the vent, and then we took off.

We arrived at the vent less than two seconds later. The butler collected her hand luggage and thanked me for a safe flight. Placing her left hand on my chest, she cocked her head back, opened her mouth, and pulled a neon green key from within. We licked the saliva off together. She used it to open the vent. I'd never known a vent to require a key before.

After the butler had lubricated my naked body to perfection, I slid into the vent with only my handbag and my wristwatch.

The End of the Vent

I fell approximately six inches from the vent to the floor.

The End of the Earth

The glass housing showed the Earth, a black ball. As the sun peered over the top, its energy whispered a golden truth: Marlon would never again see its glory.

There she appeared on a beam of perfect natural light, holding the sins of her past like giant orbs. In this moment, she was the eternal gaze of space, time, and all in the interim.

climb the ladder >>> remove the ladder >>> levitate

The planet had become a giant sheet of framed paper, unquestionable. She frowned, arms outstretched to the side, head tilted. The green and red orb surrounding her pulsated. She transcended all.

"So you *are* the murderer I'm looking for?"

"...how, exactly, did you become a detective?"

"Several days of hard training."

"I'm not convinced you attended day one."

"Are you...?"

"I would never."

"I did attend day one. It was orientation."

She floated toward me until we were nose to nose. Her breath smelled like freshly spun candy floss. "Would you like to know why I murdered all those people?"

I pulled a flip journal from my handbag. "Tell me everything."

"I did it... for you."

"For me?"

Her lizard-like tongue flicked out at my lips. "For us. I did it for us."

I tried to recall our connection. She scaled a finger down the Japanese lettering tattooed on my left pectoral muscle. "What does this mean?"

"I... I don't know. I don't speak Japanese."

She continued to caress my pectoral region. "You see, Ted torX, we share a brief, yet intimate relationship..."

"I don't follow."

She pulled my face to hers. My human tongue tangled with her snake-like variation. Her limbs twisted around mine.

She whispered, "I've witnessed your credentials."

"Who hasn't?" I replied.

She leaned back and laughed aloud.

"Oh, Tedwin torX, Jr. You are a funny goose."

I untangled my limbs. "Look... just tell me who you are!"

Her eyes took a nosedive deep into the nether regions of my soul. I trembled in the glow of infinite truth. Her lips caressed my earlobes, her sounds penetrated: a whisper.

"I am the ultimate third party."

Infinity Quest

We climbed into the enclosed space. Red lighting allowed the coordinates to be entered.

"ESCAPE POD: ACTIVATED. PREPARE TO DISEMBARK."

The red lighting turned blue. We held hands as the pod dropped into the expanding hydrogenous vacuum.

"ENGAGiNG TURBO THRUSTERS IN: THREE, TWO, ONE…"

Our latticed fingers clasped, vice-like.

I held the pill between my index finger and thumb.

"It'll be painless, this way."

We swallowed the pills with our respective saliva.

"How close will this pod get us? I mean, at what point will we burn up?"

"The radiation will kill us long before then."

"But there will be no pain, right?"

A simple smile eased my concerns. My extremities began to lose sensation. Our fingers released. The colours in the pod danced and shimmered. The screen display showed a green dotted line against a black background. It tracked our path around, and away from, planet Earth.

The green light ghosted in the faint blue haze. The green light mixed with the blue light then became enveloped by an eternal white.

> *you can query our tangibles*
> *you can oppose a vertical leap*
> *you can debate my expanding waistline*
> *but you do **not** question the résumé*

Printed in Great Britain
by Amazon